D1451019

50 Skills You Need

for a

Decent Chance of Success

Brant D. Baker

Cover Art: Daniel Escoto
V2

ISBN-13: 978-1495966927
ISBN-10: 1495966925

Dedicated to David B.
who helped me to see
just how complicated life is
for someone who doesn't have
the skills they need

Contents

50 skills you need

50 Skills You Need

DISCIPLINE

KEEP A CALENDAR*[1]

Be on time

Prioritize

Do hard and unpleasant things first

Keep track of important papers

Manage your emotions

Look both ways when you cross the street

Pick up after yourself

Obey the law

Relax now and then

Learn from your mistakes

GET 8 HOURS*

Drink plenty of water

Eat what you need, not what you don't

Floss your teeth

Do your push ups

Take a bath

---

[1] One of the *Big Five*

Wear deodorant.

Wash your hands

Take out the trash

KEEP A BUDGET*

Control your spending

Learn to save

Take care of the stuff you have

Appreciate work

FORGIVE*

Smile

Tell the truth

Say "I love you" often

Keep your promises

Make eye contact

Extend a sincere greeting

Speak when spoken to

Do unto others as you would have them do unto you

Don't gossip

Communicate

Share

Do no harm

Apologize when you are wrong

PRAY*

Give your worries to God

Be thankful in good times and challenging times.

Remain still

Accept God's amazing grace

Never stop being amazed

Never stop being curious

Read

Give back

Receive hope

Introduction

I meet broken people every day. People who have been crushed by the wheel of life, people who have been thrown off the cliff by society, people who have been broken by their boss, their parents, their ex, or just by being a person on planet earth.

I end up doing a fair amount of counseling with broken people, and as a counselor I end up doing a fair amount of life coaching. Over and over again, as people come seeking help in whatever area of their life, as we talk and pray and ponder, it seems that we often need to "get back to basics" in some way or another. This probably shouldn't come as a surprise: almost every complex endeavor is built on a foundation of fundamentals, building block skills that form the basis for more advanced performance. Almost any coach will take the time to make sure an athlete has the right grip, stance, stride, or move. Without the basics you simply can't progress to more advanced levels of competence.

All this got me to thinking about the basic skills for a balanced and successful life. The definition of "balance" and "success" will vary, and there are certainly people who have had some kind of success without being at all balanced, but they would be the outliers, the exceptions. For every reclusive, compulsive inventor or artist there are thousands upon thousands of people just trying to get through the week and raise their kids. For every Wall Street shark or professional athlete there are tens of thousands of us who are simply trying to balance our checkbook and stay in halfway decent shape.

Whatever "success" and "normal" might look like is the opposite of being broken. And no matter how unique and counter culture you might think yourself to be, you still need some basic life skills if only to function. Bottom line: most of us, whether we like it or not, are probably more normal and everyday than we'd like to believe.

I sat down and made a list, coming up with about twenty five basic practices which, to my mind, were the fundamentals of a somewhat balanced and successful life. I shared the list with my wife who added a few more, then I posted it on Facebook and invited my friends there to add their ideas. I didn't take all of their suggestions, but in the end there came to be a list of fifty fundamental skills, grouped into five categories: Faith, Finances, Responsibility, Relationships, and Health. Each of these has a list of practices that are basic to living a reasonably productive and normal life, and if something is out of kilter in your life, this list is a good quick check to see if what is wrong is something relatively easy to fix.

> *No matter how unique and counter culture you might think yourself to be, you still need some basic life skills if only to function.*

Consider what happened to Tyson. Sometime in the fall of the year he realized that something was wrong in his life but couldn't quite put his finger on what it was. His girlfriend was more and more upset with him, as was his boss, and both because he seemed to be sick quite often, missing work and missing social engagements as a result. As we talked about what might be behind this change (he had been previously a fairly healthy individual) we discovered that he wasn't really sleeping all that well, and in fact hadn't been for quite a while. How long? Well, probably since the previous winter, maybe January or February. Okay, had there been some change in his sleeping environment? No. Change in diet? Not really. Change of routine? Well, he wasn't getting quite as much exercise as he used to. And why was that? Turns out he had received a very engaging video game for Christmas, and now instead of running just before bed (his previous practice), he often as not spent an hour playing the game. This in turn tended to flood his body with adrenaline and testosterone, which then made it difficult for him to fall asleep right away. Tyson changed his routine, found a better balance, and within a few months had his health back and had restored the relationships with both boss and girlfriend.

It turns out getting eight hours of sleep is one of the *Big Five.* And so, while all 50 skills on the list are important, there is one that is absolutely essential, and five others without which getting to the others will be almost impossible. Getting eight hours, or something close to it, is absolutely essential for all but a very small handful of people. Our bodies and bodies require sleep to repair and restore, and our spirit too requires rest from a life that is too often harsh and cruel.

According to Timothy Morgenthaler, M.D, the amount of sleep we need depends on a number of factors, not least of which is our age. Infants and toddlers do best with 9-10 hours a night plus 2-3 hours of naps. School age children and teens do well with 9-11 hours, and adults, 7-8 hours. Health issues play a part, as does aging, which can trigger a change in sleeping patterns such that the needed hours may not come in a single block of time. Says Dr. Morgenthaler, "Although some people claim to feel rested on just a few hours of sleep a night, research shows that people who sleep so little over many nights don't perform as well on complex mental tasks as do people who get closer to seven hours of sleep a night. Studies among adults also show that getting less or much more than seven hours of sleep a night is associated with a higher mortality rate."[2]

Chances are you already have many of the following skills in hand. Nothing in what follows is some mysterious ancient secret or cutting edge discovery. The purpose is to have a check list, a corrective, for when things in life start to wobble. Reading through this list you may suddenly see one or two things in your life that have gotten out of balance, but hopefully you'll also be affirmed in many things that you are doing right!

---

[2] www.mayoclinic.org/how-many-hours-of-sleep-are-enough/expert-answers/FAQ-20056898

THE ONE ESSENTIAL SKILL

1) *Discipline*

There is one essential skill that precedes all the others: at some level most of the skills we'll discuss end up having something to do with *discipline*. *Discipline always seems painful in the moment*, which is probably why many people seek to avoid it altogether, but it turns out that discipline is one of the most essential skills a person can learn.

Discipline has to do with *foresight*, the ability to imagine a future and then delay short-term gratifications in order to reach that future goal. What most of the other 49 life skills represent is an expression of disciple, or in some cases a pathway to it.

So, arranging your life to ensure something close to 8 hours of sleep means giving up on other enticements of the moment: to stay up late playing video games, or watching movies, or going out to parties, or idly scanning social media. This takes discipline, it takes determination, it takes having a long-term goal of living a healthier life over the short-term goal of beating last night's best game score. Turning off the video game, or the movie, or the social media won't guarantee either a great night's sleep or a life time of improved physical and mental health, but *not* turning them off probably guarantees the opposite.

> *Discipline always seems painful in the moment, which is probably why many people seek to avoid it altogether. But it turns out that discipline has to do with foresight...*

Discipline, and specifically self-discipline is a skill that few people naturally possess. In an excellent paper on the subject (later published and available on Amazon), Theodore Bryant compares discipline to a muscle. For much of our lives other people (parents, teachers, bosses) provide us with discipline (control, if you prefer) and so we are not required to exercise this muscle for ourselves, which then causes it to grow flabby and weak. Furthermore, there is a part of us (he likens this part to Mr. Hyde in Robert Louis Stevenson's classic *Dr. Jekyll and Mr. Hyde*) who seeks to resist control of any sort (that is, from either inside or outside ourselves). "Regardless of whether you're trying to stay on a diet, clean out the garage, or be more productive in your occupation," says Bryant, "the secret to success revolves around your ability to recognize and deal with the part of you that offers resistance... Then, in situations where we are called upon to be our own boss, we seem powerless to overcome contrary inner influences, both conscious and subconscious... [and] the part of us that doesn't want to be disciplined takes control of our behavior (45-46).

The good news is that self-discipline is a skill that can be learned, a muscle that can be developed. But to do so we need to first deal with a collection of attitudes, fears, and myths that impede our progress.

The strength of Bryant's work is its recognition of this psychological part of the process, common struggles like:

- What's the point of all of this? (Cynicism) - Corrective: "Believe in your ability to improve" (16).

- Why bother? (Negativism) - Corrective: "Believe that your attitude has everything to do with your success" (19).

- I'm not good enough (Defeatism) - Corrective: "Don't lament over your shortcomings, redouble your efforts" (22).

- Let's go do something else (Escapism) - Corrective: "Believe that life, for the most part, is based on the cause-and-effect principle" (25).

- We'll do it later (Delayism) - Corrective: "Recognize whether the delay is working for you or against you" (27).

- Fear of Failure - Corrective: recognize that humiliation is most likely the root problem here and remind ourselves "that failure is not humiliation unless we make it so in our own minds. Failure can be viewed as a stepping stone rather than a tombstone. Once this reality is fully accepted, fear of failure loses its power to sabotage our self-discipline" (57).

- Fear of Success – Corrective: recognize that this fear likely originates in either feelings of low self-esteem or feelings of guilt. It may be we need to spend time analyzing past successes to see if they really turned out as "badly" as we imagine (63).

> The department manager was a wise, if succinct man, who, during an interview was asked, "Sir, what is the secret of your success?"
>
> He said, "Two words: right decisions."
>
> "And sir how do you make right decisions?"
>
> "One word," he responded, "experience."
>
> "And sir, how do you get experience?"
>
> "Two words: wrong decisions."

- Fear of Rejection – Corrective: examine yourself to learn if this fear is related to your desire to be perceived as a "nice person," and if therefore you spend too much time and energy trying to satisfy others, thus damaging your ability to pursue the things you want or need to do (71).

- Fear of Mediocrity – Corrective: seek to understand if this fear is actually a mask for perfectionism, which in turn creates a barrier through self-imposed pressure, which in turn can cause us to avoid doing things that may lead to failure, and in the end causing a failure of self-discipline (76).

- Fear of Risks – Corrective: examine yourself to learn if you might actually doubt your ability to succeed in unfamiliar situations. "When self-doubt intrudes your self-discipline effort never receives the very important 'I can do it' message that supports its growth" (80).

Bryant gives several days' worth of exercises to overcome each of these, and that alone is worth the price of the book! He then goes on to review the four basic stages in the process of self-discipline.

1) The decision to act

"During the Decision Stage your purpose is to build a psychological foundation, a commitment that will carry you through all the steps (hourly, daily, weekly, monthly) that your goal requires. A solid psychological foundation will empower you to deal with all the doubts, fears, and self-defeating beliefs that Hyde will send your way (hourly, daily, weekly, monthly). Ironically, the more important your goal is to you, the more Hyde will try to keep you from going after it. For Hyde, you see, an important goal appears frightening and difficult. Because of this, you will need to be aware of Hyde every step of the way. Self-discipline is easier when you know exactly what you are up against" (138).

2) Preparation

"Traveling from your desires to your goals, you will always need to go through a series of steps. So, when you decide to make the trip, preparation is a necessary piece of luggage. Preparing for action means that you need to make a *daily* plan. Your plan will, of course, contain steps that need to be accomplished by certain times and dates. Without question, self-discipline flows much better when you receive daily reminders about what to do and when to do it. Moreover, self-discipline works better if the reminders are written onto paper rather than left floating in your head. All we are talking about here is a simple "to do" list. And, most important, if your written list breaks each task into small steps, you will find that your resistance to doing each task greatly diminishes.

"Remember: Every daily plan needs to be a *simple* plan, an uncomplicated "to do" list. Unless you have a written plan, Hyde will overwhelm you by subconsciously convincing you that your goal is just too big for little ol' you to accomplish. But a simple daily "to do" list reminds you that every big accomplishment is nothing more than a lot of little accomplishments added together. So, on your daily "to do" list be sure to break down each task into a series of small steps. This simple act will instantly transform intimidating tasks into friendly steps. Incidentally, this "simplifying" technique will help you get going again if you have been hit by a Hyde roadblock. Self-discipline: It's a trial by the mile and hard by the yard, but a cinch by the inch" (142-143).

3) Action

"Make a simple daily "to do" list. For your first list you can use the one you made during the Preparation Stage. Here is what makes this list different from most: Next to each step write a guess at how many minutes you plan to work on the step, not prepare for, but actually do the step. When writing your steps, always keep them small.

"Important: Remember that you are likely to *overestimate* the time needed for an unpleasant step, and *underestimate* the time needed for a pleasant step. The good news is that your uninviting steps will be over quicker than you imagined. Do one minute of relaxation before doing each step. Put a line through the step when completed. At the end of the day

take a look at your list. Reward yourself, no matter how few steps toward your goal were completed. Small steps add up fast. So thank yourself and Hyde for each completed step, then remember to place each uncompleted step on tomorrow's "to do" list. If you carry the same step more than five days maybe you need to break that step into smaller steps. Or take a look at what you are telling yourself about that step that is making it difficult for you" (149).

4) Completion/Maintenance

"Be alert! Don't let Hyde subconsciously use rationalization and justification to make you slack off on your self-discipline. Don't minimize the importance of each little step you need to take in order to get where you want to go. Use Relaxation to turn the volume up on Hyde's messages. Then you can find out *specifically* what you are telling yourself that blocks your progress. When you can hear Hyde's *specific* negative self-talk, you can counter and replace it with supportive messages (156)

Theodore Bryant's book is called *Self-Discipline in 10 Days: How to Go from Thinking to Doing*.[3] I can only add that doing his exercises and learning the skill of self-discipline in itself teaches discipline!

---

[3] HUB Publishing, all citations from the 2004 edition

BEING RESPONSIBLE

Are people responsible, or not? Well, it depends. A study on the amount of credit claimed by collaborators of jointly authored academic papers suggests that each person claimed more than one quarter of the work. In fact, on average the total credit claimed by a four-person team came to 140 percent![4]

On the other hand, if you are looking for the people or person responsible for the social ills of the day, the problems with the economy, or climate change you tend to get a lot of finger pointing. It's like the story about what happened in a small Texas town when a bar began to expand their building. The local church started a campaign to block the expansion, a campaign that included both petitions and prayers. Just before the grand opening the bar was struck by lightning and burned to the ground. The church folks were smug and bragged about the power of prayer...until the bar owner sued them for the destruction of his building. In its reply to the court, the church vehemently denied all responsibility, to which the judge said, "I don't know how I'm going to decide this, but it appears from the paperwork that we have a bar owner who believes in the power of prayer, and an entire church congregation that now does not."

The first area of skills for life has to do with *Responsibility.* Let's face it, there are a lot of things in life we can't change or control. But one of the places all of us have the *most* control is over ourselves. Take responsibility for yourself and a lot of other things will fall into place.

2) *KEEP A CALENDAR**
The first of the *Big Five.* In addition to the *Big One* (the skill of discipline) the *Big Five* are pretty much non-negotiable

---

[4] Robert Wright, "Why Can't We All Just Get Along? The Uncertain Biological Basis of Morality" *Atlantic Monthly*, November 2013, 110

skills and prerequisite skills, without which any talk about the remaining skills in any area is likely to be just talk. It's amazing how many people believe they can keep track of their lives in their head, and they have just enough success in doing so to marginally prove the myth. But while a lot of folks live in fairly simple and straightforward ways, the truth is that certain infrequent events are best tracked through some kind of calendar. Things like doctor and dental appointments are obvious; things like when to change the air filters in your house or rotate the tires on your car, less so.

A wise man I once knew liked to say, "You can always make more money, but you can't make more time." Time is the ultimate precious resource, and one we are most likely to take for granted: it appears to be renewable, but in fact it is finite. All of us are given the same twenty-four hours, no more, no less. And then there is the reality that someday our time will end. The Bible says that God eventually turns us all back to dust, that our lives are swept away like a dream, like grass that is fresh in the morning, but which in the evening fades and withers. The days of our life are seventy years, or perhaps eighty if we are strong, or perhaps even ninety if we have a good medical plan, but sooner or later they are gone and we fly away. So what can we do? "Teach us to count our days," says the Psalmist, that we may gain a wise heart" (Psalm 90:3-5, 10, 12).

> A wise man I once knew liked to say, "You can make more money, but you can't make more time."

The life skill of keeping a calendar reminds us not only of our ultimate finite nature, but helps us wisely use the valuable time we have. Remember the old idea of how much water you waste if you have a dripping faucet? (Answer: 1,440 drips per day, or 34 gallons a year, according to the US Geological Survey Water Science School). Now turn the drips into seconds. If you waste 1440 seconds a day (a ridiculous unit of measurement, but work with me here), that translates into 24 minutes a day. A lot of people will spend that much time and more idly wandering through the Internet. Do that every day all year long and you will have dripped away 8,760 minutes, which equals 146 hours, or almost four work weeks.

I'm not arguing for all of us to become time sergeants. There's definitely a time and place for relaxation (see below). But most people I know probably get more relaxation than they need, and many of those have been known to sit around in their leisure and complain about the way the world is going. What if, instead of dripping away nearly a half hour every day (and likely quite a bit more if we're honest), we invested in social capital? What if you collected all those drops of time and gave them to someone who was thirsty, or used them to water our collective garden? What if we all spent just an hour a week helping to alleviate loneliness or hunger or illiteracy or homelessness or any of a dozen social ills that plague us all? After all, it's not just the other guy's end of the boat that is sinking...

The first step to capturing those dripping minutes is understanding how you use your time. A calendar might be called a "time budget." You need to know what you spend so you can more clearly see what is being wasted and what might be saved. And just like a financial budget, it's not enough to simply plug things in and then ignore it. A calendar does its best work for you when you take five minutes every day or so to manage it. Appointments get changed, some things end up taking more time, some less, life happens and you must respond. Please spare us all some lame complaint like, "I don't have time to keep or manage a calendar..." If you even think that's true then you obviously don't have time not to!

3) **Be on time**

Being late, especially if you are meeting someone, can really be a kind of selfishness, a way of saying that your time is more important than the other person's time. Sure unexpected delays come to us all, but if you have a cross-town appointment at 5:00pm and you don't leave until 4:45, please don't blame the traffic when you come in fifteen minutes late: have the courage to blame yourself and then apologize. Wasting your own time is one thing, wasting someone else's should be a punishable offence!

4) **Prioritize**

Deciding what to do first and what can wait is a basic proficiency that isn't too hard to learn. Paying attention to these 50 skills for life is a good place to start. Relationships, finances, responsibility, health and faith are important things to take care of first, then fit other things in around those. A corollary to this life skill is to understand when you are best at doing certain tasks. I am a morning person, and as a pastor writing sermons is one of the big demands on my time and energy, so I block out two hours first thing on my calendar every morning to write. Conversely, I am pretty much brain dead by 4:00 in the afternoon, but my body is crying out for attention, so that's when I go to the gym. Knowing when you have the best energy, when you are at your peak for a given part of your life, is helpful when setting up priorities.

5) **Do hard and unpleasant things first**

It's amazing how much *emotional* energy an unpleasant task can sap away from us, which means the longer we avoid doing it the less effective we are doing whatever it is we are using as an excuse to not do it, and the less we're enjoying it. A corollary to this life skill is "only touch things once." In other words, if you open a piece a mail that is going to require you go upstairs and dig through your files, go. *Do not* throw the mail into the stack of "things you intend to get to real soon" because it takes too much effort to go upstairs.

It's in your hand and so do it now if you possibly can. It often takes twice as much energy and effort to get back into something than to just take care of it when it is in front of you.

Champion golfer Greg Norman has said that one of the best pieces of advice he ever got was from his first coach who would say "DIN and DIP," do it now, and do it proper.[5]

> One of the best pieces of advice Greg Norman ever got was from his first coach who would say "DIN and DIP," do it now, and do it proper."

6) *Keep track of important papers*

It could be as simple as a file folder marked "Important Papers" (I have one of those) where you keep your birth certificate, your social security card, your passport, and maybe a handful of other basic life documents (such as all of the above for your children if you have any). Tax files (federal, state, property), insurance documents (home, auto), bank statements, retirement accounts, legal and loan documents, and so forth are all things the average person needs from time to time. Spending two minutes to put a bank statement away in the right place could save you fifteen minutes of pawing through a pile of papers later.

7) *Manage your emotions*

According to Darlene Mininni (Ph.D, MPH), author of *The Emotional Toolkit,* all emotions fall into four categories: anxiety, sadness, anger and happiness. The first step in managing emotions is to identify what exactly you are feeling. To do that Mininni offers a series of questions

- •Is there something I'm afraid of? (anxiety)
- •Is there something that I've lost? (sadness)

---

[5] *Golf Magazine,* "The Book of Norman," 62, January 2014

•Have I been attacked in some way? (anger)
•Have I gained something? (happiness)

Having identified the emotion you are in position to take action, so see what you can do to resolve the situation. If there is no apparent or immediate resolution then turn to your emotional toolkit. In that toolkit are healthy strategies you have developed to cope with negative emotions: exercise, talking with a close friend, prayer or meditation, journaling, or (to a limited degree) seeking out enjoyable distraction (but careful here to make sure that the distraction doesn't become a primary way of avoiding emotions and the problems that underlie them).[6]

8) *Look both ways when you cross the street*
Yes, this is meant both literally and metaphorically.

9) *Pick up after yourself*
Really, you think your mother is going to come over and clean that up? Do it, and do it when you make the mess ("I'll clean that up later" is a mantra of failure).

10) *Obey the law*
Don't be like the two men in Kentucky who tried to pull off the front of a cash machine by running a chain from the machine to the bumper of their pickup truck. Instead of pulling the front panel off the machine, they pulled the bumper off their truck, which scared them so much they left the scene of the crime...and left the chain still attached to the machine....with their bumper still attached to the chain...with their vehicle's license plate still attached to the bumper. Or how about the woman in Arizona who called "Guns For Hire," a company that stages gunfights for Western movies and so forth, because she wanted to have her husband killed. Instead she got 5 years. Obey the law.

---

[6] www.psychcentral.com/blog/archives/2012/07/03/how-to-manage-emotions-more-effectively.

11) *Relax now and then*

Being responsible means having a counterweight to robustly managing our time, so take time out to relax and enjoy a hobby or two!

12) *Learn from your mistakes*

Defeat does not mean failure. Booker T. Washington said, "Success is to be measured not so much by the position that one has reached in life as by the obstacles which he has overcome while trying to succeed." Sometimes life is two steps forward, one step back, but the overall direction is still toward the goal. History is full of stories of people who overcame their mistakes and backwards steps to move on. "Abraham Lincoln ran for political office seven times and was defeated each time. Bobby Kennedy failed third grade and could not even take care of his own paper route. Babe Ruth struck out more times than any other baseball player. Ed Gibson, one of the astronauts on the Skylab III mission, failed first and fourth grades" (*The Complete Book of Home Management*, Elva Anson and Kathie Liden, Moody Press, 1985).

Please note that all this assumes you will make mistakes. Making mistakes is a requirement of life—by which I mean true mistakes, those errors of action or judgment based mostly in ignorance, as opposed to acts of defiance, disruption, or deviousness. Some mistakes are more costly than others, but at the end of the day the real sin is to not learn from them.

So be responsible, but don't live like the purpose of life is to arrive safely at death... Don't let fear dictate your decisions and don't stop making mistakes. Stop pointing out problems and use your time to be part of the solution.[7]

---

[7] *Wild Goose Chase: Reclaim the Adventure of Pursuing God*, Mark Batterson, Multnomah Books, 2008

BEING HEALTHLY

An 85-year-old couple, married almost 60 years, had enjoyed good health for most of their lives thanks primarily to the wife's interest in health food and exercise. But one day their time came as the result of a car crash. When they reached the pearly gates, St. Peter took them to their mansion, which was decked out with a beautiful kitchen, an impressive master suite, and a hot tub.

As they "oohed" and "aahed," the old man asked Peter how much all this was going to cost. "It's free," Peter replied, "This is Heaven."

Next they went out back to survey the championship golf course that the home overlooked. Each week the course changed, explained Peter, to a new one representing the great golf courses on earth.

The old man asked, "What are the green fees?"

Peter's reply, "This is Heaven! You play for free."

Next they went to the clubhouse and saw a lavish buffet lunch with the foods of the world laid out in abundance.

"How much to eat?" asked the old man.

"Don't you understand yet? This is Heaven, it's free!" Peter replied with some exasperation.

"Well, where are the low fat and low cholesterol tables?" the old man asked timidly.

Peter explained, "That's the best part--you can eat as much as you like of whatever you like and you never get fat and you never get sick. This is Heaven!"

With that the old man went into a fit of anger, throwing down his hat, stomping his feet, and shrieking wildly. Peter and his wife both tried to calm him down, asking him what was wrong. The old man looked at his wife and said, "This is all your fault! If it weren't for your blasted bran muffins, I could have been here ten years ago!"

The next area of skills for successfully navigating life is in the area of health. This is one of those areas where most of us have more control than not. Genetics notwithstanding, *you* are in control of what you eat, how much you exercise, and how much you sleep.

13) ***GET 8 HOURS****
One of the *Big Five* for sure!

According to Dr. Timothy Morgenthaler, the amount of sleep we need depends on a number of factors, not least of which is our age. Infants and toddlers do best with 9-10 hours a night plus 2-3 hours of naps. School age children and teens do well with 9-11 hours, and adults, 7-8 hours. Health issues play a part, as does aging, which can trigger a change in sleeping patterns such that the needed hours may not come in a single block of time. In other words, senior citizens may only sleep six hours at night, but then nap a bit in the afternoon or after dinner, perhaps cleverly disguising their nap as watching educational television programming. Says Dr. Morgenthaler, "Although some people claim to feel rested on just a few hours of sleep a night, research shows that people who sleep so little over many nights don't perform as well on complex mental tasks as do people who get closer to seven hours of sleep a night. Studies among adults also show that getting less or much more than seven hours of sleep a night is associated with a higher mortality rate."[8] In other words, you aren't superman, and you will pay the price—physically, emotionally, and in terms of performance—if you don't pay attention to your sleep.

14) ***Drink plenty of water***
Almost as important as getting enough sleep is getting enough H_2O. According to the website *lifehack.org,* drinking plenty of water helps improve mental ability, improves

---

[8] www.mayoclinic.org/how-many-hours-of-sleep-are-enough/expert-answers/FAQ-20057898

physical performance, lessens fatigue, helps expel toxins, helps you lose weight (especially if you drink water instead of a sugary drink), helps reduce the risk of heart attacks and stroke, improves digestion, and decreases certain cancers.[9]

15) *Eat what you need, not what you don't*
Another way to put this is to "Eat a colorful variety of real, whole foods from real ingredients that you can make yourself...food that comes from a farmer's field rather than a factory, food that traveled the shortest distance from the field to your fork—that is what we should eat."[10]

Even people who aren't into auto mechanics know that you have to put the right fuel into your car. If you instead put in soda or grease, or pretty much anything else, your car isn't going to run. Why then are we so careless about what we put into our bodies? And if you think a car, with its 10,000 parts, is complex, then what about your body, with its trillions of cells? The food we eat is the fuel for a complex and amazing machine that doesn't deserve to be junked up! There are lots of great books out there, including *The Daniel Plan,* that offer sensible, well-balanced diets and nutrition advice. Go eat one up!

By-the-way, not only what we eat but who we eat with is important. Research has consistently shown that the more often families eat together the less likely their children will smoke, drink, use drugs, have sex at a young age or get into fights. Frequent family dining also contributes to children doing well in school and developing healthy eating habits. These correlations are true regardless of a teen's gender, family structure or socioeconomic level.[11]

---

[9] lifehack.org/articles/lifestyle/7-awesome-reasons-why-you-should-drink-more-water.html
[10] *The Daniel Plan,* 74-75
[11] *Christian Century,* September 20, 2003, p 7

16) **Floss your teeth**

Every time you see your dental hygienist ...and note here the assumption you *are* making regular visits...they will ask if you are flossing your teeth. Why? Because even more than brushing, flossing is a proven way to improve and preserve oral health. If you don't take care of your teeth then you won't want to eat, and when you don't eat you won't stay healthy. Plus, there is intriguing evidence that connects periodontal disease with heart disease. Researchers aren't sure why, but it's just one more reason to take care of your teeth!

17) **Do your push ups**

One day a man said to his neighbor, "You look tired." Yes, said the other man, "I just finished doing 50 push-ups." "Oh really?" asked the neighbor, "When did you start doing push-ups?" "Well," said the man, "I did the first one in 1986."

We laugh, but a basic life skill is to do *something* to stay in shape (not necessarily push ups). Doing even 15 minutes a day is better than doing nothing. A simple routine of push-ups, jumping jacks (about 10 calories a minute...roughly equal to many good cardio work-outs), and some kind abdominal exercise (like sit ups) can be done at home and without any equipment whatsoever. More involved and intensive workouts are easy to come by, but the point is to *get moving.* According to a list found in *The Daniel Plan,* exercise is the best strategy to increase energy, improve muscular strength, improve muscle tone and endurance, and strengthen your bones. It will increase your joint mobility, which will help you manage

> Exercise will make you look and feel younger, increase your productivity, and stimulate your creativity, and make you happier, by reducing stress, anxiety and depression.

your weight, and of course it will decrease your body fat. These in turn will enhance your immune function and help prevent more than forty chronic diseases including heart disease, stroke, cancer, high blood pressure, diabetes, and joint problems. Exercise will make you look and feel younger, increase your productivity, and stimulate your creativity, and make you happier, by reducing stress, anxiety and depression. It will sharpen your focus, promote restful sleep, and enhance intimacy and relationships make you smarter, and improve your posture.[12] So consult with you doctor and then *move it*!

18) *Take a bath* and 19) *Wear deodorant*.
Note that these aren't necessarily only for your benefit.

20) *Wash your hands*
According to the Centers for Disease Control and Prevention, hand washing is one of the easiest and simplest ways to keep people healthy. Germs spread from hands to objects (phones, pens, elevator buttons, handrails, tabletops, toys) and then to other people as they touch their eyes, nose and mouth without even realizing it. Handwashing reduces respiratory illness in the general population by 21%, and reduces the number of people who get sick with diarrhea by 31%. Don't be that guy who leaves the restroom without washing his hands, or that mom who doesn't wash her hands before helping to feed her children, because not washing hands is particularly harmful to children, killing about 2.2 million children under the age of 5 each year from various diseases. Moreover, good handwashing early in life may help improve child development in some settings.[13]

21) *Take out the trash*
Of course we have to take out the trash because if we don't

---

[12] *The Daniel Plan*, 41
[13] www.cdc.gov/handwashing/ why-handwashing.html

it will pile up. The life skill here, however, is more than practical in nature. For one thing, taking out the trash is one of life's many chores. Chores have to get done, and the sooner the better (see above **Do hard and unpleasant things first** and **Pick up after yourself**). People who shirk chores, or worse, who argue with their spouse or roommate about whose turn it is, are in danger of missing the point that chores are part of life.

But of course there is also metaphorical trash that needs to be taken out as well. Every life and every relationship accumulates a certain amount of trash. People hurt us, we hurt other people, stuff happens. Pretty soon, if we don't take out the trash, life will start to stink and may even attract unpleasant vermin. The life skill of taking out this metaphor-ical trash will be covered below: it is called **Forgiveness** and it is the first of the *Big Five* in the *Relationships* section. Learn to forgive—it's an acquired skill, not something any of us do naturally—and you will help keep your life from accumulating a lot of trash.

FINANCE BASICS

Have you heard about the redneck cowboy from Texas who walked into a bank in New York City and asked for a loan? He told the loan officer that he was going to Paris for the International Redneck Festival and would be gone for two weeks. He needed to borrow $5,000 but he was not a depositor at that bank.

The bank officer told him that the bank would need some form of security for the loan, so the Redneck handed over the keys to a new Ferrari. The car was parked on the street in front of the bank. He produced the title and everything checked out. The loan officer agreed to hold the car as collateral for the loan and apologized for having to charge 12% interest. Later, the bank's president and its officers all enjoyed a good laugh at the Redneck from Texas for using a $250,000 Ferrari as collateral for a $5,000 loan. An employee of the bank then drove the Ferrari into the bank's underground garage and parked it.

Two weeks later, the Redneck returned, repaid the $5,000 and the interest of $23.07. The loan officer said, "Sir, we are very happy to have had your business, and this transaction has worked out very nicely, but we are a little puzzled. While you were away, we checked you out on Dun & Bradstreet and found that you are a highly successful investor and multimillionaire with real estate and financial interests all over the world. Your investments include a large number of wind turbines around Sweetwater, Texas. What puzzles us is why you would bother to borrow $5,000?" The good ol' Texas boy replied, "Where else in New York City can I park my car for two weeks for only $23.07 and expect it to be here when I return?"

We may not all be this cagey, but there are a few things anyone can do to improve their skills in the area of finances. And here again, this is one area that many of us have more control than we tend to think, starting with your ability to...

22) *KEEP A BUDGET**

Another one of the *Big Five* so don't ignore it!

Let's face it: no matter how much we make, there's never enough. That being the case, we'd best learn how to manage what we do have, which is why keeping a budget is one of the *Big Five*. Probably 90% of the couples who come to me for marital counseling sooner or later get around to mentioning money as part of their problem. When I ask, I find that very few of these families have a family budget.

> Probably 90% of the couples who come to me for marital counseling get around to mentioning money as part of their problem. When I ask, I find that very few of these families have a family budget.

A few practical strategies here include doing an annual budget. Too many families, if they do budget, only budget monthly. But car and house repairs, dentist and doctor visits, and many other expensive parts of our lives don't happen every month. Sit down and figure out an annual budget.

And as you do, be honest and be thorough. If it is part of your life style to eat your lunch out every day, then budget for it. I was talking to a couple once who ate out lunch every day. He said, "Well, we only spend about five bucks." I then turned to her, and she said, "Yeah, me too." Then they said they went out to dinner about once a week, spending about $30.00 on that. We did the math and discovered they were spending about $4,000 a year on eating out. Their eyes got big as I suggested to them that, it was fine if they had that kind of money, but by putting it in a family budget they'd at least have a choice about whether or not that's how they wanted to spend the four grand!

Finally, designate someone in the family to track expenses and compare them to the budget. Watching things month to month will help you avoid surprises. Yes, it may be true that you have $500 budgeted for vacation, but did you notice that your phone bill is through the roof, or that gas prices have toasted that line item? Keeping up with things month to month will keep you from making wrong assumptions that can lead to overspending.

Which, by-the-way, has its own cost. Financial experts say that overspending can cost you as much as $1,200 each year in late charges and penalties. If you were able to avoid those costs and instead invest the $1,200 every year with compounding interest, you'd have $94,870 in your pocket![14]

Be honest and be thorough, and your family budget will be a helpful tool. It won't magically fix your money woes but it will go a long way toward helping you make intelligent choices. It will also go a long way toward avoiding the family fights and marital unhappiness that comes from financial pressure.

23) *Control your spending*

Consider the garnish. In 1992, Delta Airlines decided to quit using a single leaf of lettuce to dress up their in-flight meal trays. Passengers still got the same meals, they just didn't have the lettuce decor. They never got a single letter of complaint, but that missing lettuce ended up saving Delta about $1.5 million a year.[15]

Are there lettuce leaves in your life? The biggest might be to get out of debt if you have any. Paying someone hundreds of dollars a year on money you have borrowed, except perhaps for a house or a car, is just nuts. Use the money you find in your budget, or use money you find by otherwise

---

[14] www.bankrate.com/finance/smart-spending/bad-habits-cost-1.aspx
[15] *Houston Chronicle*, 3/24/96, p.9D

controlling your spending, to pay down short term loans ASAP. Giving up a couple of colas a week, or a pizza or two each month might get you going. Review your cell phone and cable plans for cute features that you really don't need or use. Take two minutes to clip enough grocery coupons to save two dollars a week and have an extra $100 in your pocket by the end of the year. Spend an hour one weekend to do an auto and home insurance review and you might be surprised. There
are a lot of ways that money leaks through our hands: the skill here is to be alert to what is happening and plug those holes!

24) *Learn to save*

It's never easy, because there is hardly ever enough just to make it through the year, but if you will make, and keep a budget, and if you'll learn to control your spending, chances are you'll find at least a few dollars to save each month. If you could save just $50 monthly and invest it over thirty years with compounding interest you would have almost $50,000 by the time those years had passed.

Of course, there are different kinds of savings. Saving for retirement is important and something you'll thank yourself for later in life, but saving for emergencies is equally critical. When unexpected things happen in life, and they always do, having something put away not only gives you more choices but also peace of mind. The kind of short term loans that get most people in trouble (usually in the way of credit card debt) can be avoided if you've got cash at the ready. Save it now or pay someone else for a long time later: the choice is yours!

25) *Take care of the stuff you have*

I'm always amazed at the things people lose, or damage, or throw away because fixing them seems too much of a hassle, or whatever. The stuff sitting in our church lost-and-found defies any rational explanation. I mean, really, how do you lose a shoe and not notice? Clothes seem to be the thing that people misplace most often. Clothes and sun glasses. And water bottles—we have a lot of water bottles.

I get that we're all busy and distracted, but think of this in terms of a time-money analysis: you're busy and distracted because one of the things you're trying to manage in your life is work and the needs you have to make a living. But if you lose the sweater you just paid for last week because you're so busy replying to e-mail on your phone, have you really gained anything? Take care of the stuff you already worked for and then you can work for other things, like saving for retirement, when you will probably need that sweater.

26) *Appreciate work*

In his Rule of 1223, St. Francis speaks of "the grace of working." Work is a grace in general, and having a job is a gift in particular. Value your work. Don't be a lazybones, who sleeps and waits and procrastinates, or worse, who quits a job without any prospects because he is bored or thinks the job is beneath him or just doesn't

> Work is a grace in general, and having a job is a gift in particular. Value your work.

feel like working. Be more like the ant, who according to Proverbs 6, is wise in working without having to be prodded to do it, preparing and laying in supplies all summer long.

Lisa Van Oyen once surveyed a group of colleagues and students, asking about the benefits of work.[16] Responses included:

---

[16] *Financial Intelligence*, ABC Radio, Goldfields, Western Australia, Saturday 16 July 2011

- Understanding the time and effort traded for the particular item and so the value of money
- Understanding over time that it is better to receive a higher amount per hour for less effort and this usually requires the sacrifice of further education
- Understanding parental sacrifice and point of view
- Learning skills
- Increases self-esteem
- Gives a sense of achievement
- Prepares you for later in life
- Learning how money can be handled and mishandled
- Opportunity to earn money and give gifts to others
- Opportunity to learn time management
- Learning to do things you don't want to do
- Taking responsibility
- Being able to buy yourself rewards

I agree. I have seen firsthand what an absolutely wonderful gift work can be as it not only provides for families financially but also helps order life, offers social interaction, and can generate a sense of value and self-worth. This isn't to glorify work beyond what it is: it's work, I get it.

But not working is generally not a happy thing. I help lead a group called *For Our City*. It's a group that represents leaders from non-profits, businesses, churches, and the city of Mesa. A few months ago we divided ourselves into task forces to look more closely at some of the areas we are working on: education, homelessness, food, and employment. I happened to bump into a man who oversees one of the more prominent non-profit agencies in Mesa that helps feed and clothe the homeless and needy. He was headed to the employment task force, not the food task force. "A job answers many questions," he said to me in passing.

Yup, it does, so appreciate it!

RELATIONSHIPS

Relationships are an important part of our lives. According to a Barna Group survey, more than four out of every ten adults – 44% – said their top priority in life is having a satisfying family life. Women were much more likely than men to list family as their top priority (48% versus 39%, respectively) even though family was the top ranked priority among men by a three-to-one margin.[17]

> G. K. Chesterton once said, "The Bible tells us to love our neighbors, and also to love our enemies; probably because they are generally the same people."

But of course family is just one expression of our relational world. G. K. Chesterton once said, "The Bible tells us to love our neighbors, and also to love our enemies; probably because they are generally the same people."[18] The bottom line is that even the most lonely loner isn't without some kind of relation-ship, be it a neighbor, a boss, or a barber. It is probably no accident, therefore, that this set of skills is the longest!

27) *FORGIVE**

> The skill of forgiveness heads the list in the Relationship category because it is one of the *Big Five*, the skill in this group without which most of the others won't matter. As a pastor one of the things I am asked most often is how to forgive someone. It's a good question because forgiveness is a "learned skill," almost a craft, something which none of us do naturally or particularly well. There are five steps to this skill:[19]

---

[17] May, 2005

[18] *Illustrated London News*, July 16, 1910

[19] *Teaching P.R.A.Y.E.R*, Brant D. Baker, (Abingdon Press, 2001), 89f

The first step, before we can forgive anyone, or even before we can receive forgiveness from anyone, is that we **receive** forgiveness from God. I'll tell you as nicely as I know how that most people, including most Christians, still don't get it. Get what? The stunning Good News that God's forgiveness *precedes* repentance. Jesus did not wait for his outcast friends to repent and become respectable before going to dinner with them. Instead, he barged in on these sinners with the announcement that their sins had been forgiven-- before their repentance, before they did anything to make restitution, perhaps before they even realized they needed forgiving. Most of us, including most Christians don't get the fact that in Jesus Christ we are forgiven, so now we can repent. So, the first step in this skill called forgiveness is that we **receive** forgiveness.

The second step in the skill of forgiveness is to **recognize** that there is a need for it. To recognize is to pull aside the curtains that hide our anger, our guilt, our pain, and admit that there is a problem. The Bible offers some permission-giving and boundary-setting advice: "Be angry but do not sin; do not let the sun go down on your anger, and do not make room for the devil" (Ephesians 4:26). When we **recognize** we are owning the fact that we are angry--at ourselves for having sinned against God or neighbor, or at our neighbor for having sinned against us. Part of this step of **recognizing** is to be honest about who all may stand in need of forgiveness. What I mean by honesty is this: while we are usually very aware of the sins others have committed against us, it is probable that we have also sinned against others as well. There is usually much more mutuality in our relation-ships than we would like to admit. Too often our efforts at forgiveness break down because both people come ready to forgive, but not ready to be forgiven!

The next step in the skill of forgiveness is that we conduct an honest **review** of what has happened. To **review** helps us be truthful with ourselves and others as we honestly share our struggles.

The fourth step in forgiveness is something we might call "revisioning" and it is here that we get to the heart of the matter. To **revision** is to look for a vision other than the one we currently see. When we are hurt, when we have been wounded, all we can see is our anger and bitterness. The most powerful re-visioning I've ever encountered was taught to me by a woman who had been physically abused by her grandfather. She described to me a powerful vision in which she saw herself and her grandfather both being covered with blood. As she looked for the source she saw Jesus on his cross, his blood showering down on both herself and on her abuser. It was the beginning for her of being released from a lifetime of hatred and bitterness, allowing her to get on with her life. No, it didn't make it right, no, it didn't come close to avenging the heinous things done to her, it didn't even get communicated to her grandfather, but it was a vision that freed her to live.

And while we're on the subject, let me say a brief word here about forgiving "repeat offenders." A lot of damage has been done by the misguided advice that someone who is being abused must "forgive" their abuser and return to the abusive situation. Let's be clear: forgiveness does not preclude accountability nor punishment. A superficial or spiritualized notion of forgiveness that does nothing to provide a stern grace of judgment has missed the essence of what true forgiveness is all about.

> This may come as a shock, but the words, "for-give and forget" are not in the Bible.

Finally, the last step in forgiveness is to **revisit**. This may come as a shock to many of us, but the phrase, "forgive and forget" are not in the Bible. And in fact, besides being impossible for us, these words are rather poor advice. A better idea would be for us to "remember well," starting with the fact that that forgiveness is not so much an event as it is a process. Some people have been misled into believing that if they can't "forgive and forget," that if the old feelings come up again, then they have somehow failed at forgiveness. Perhaps this is part of why Jesus suggested to Peter that we are to forgive not seven times, but seventy times seven (Matthew 18:22). It's not necessarily that our offender will sin against us that many times, but more likely that we will replay the offence in our memory that many times and more! So, every time the old feelings of hurt and pain return we **revisit** our previous decision to forgive and speak those words of forgiveness once more.

28) *Smile*

Smiling has a number of benefits according to Dr. Mark Stibich, who gives ten reasons to do it. Smiling helps attract people toward us, it changes our mood, and it is contagious. Smiling relieves stress, boosts your immune system (possibly because you are more relaxed), and lowers your blood pressure (ditto). Smiling releases good stuff into our bodies like endorphins, natural pain killers, and serotonin (smiling is a natural drug!). Smiling works muscles in your face that will help you look younger, and it makes you seem more confident, successful, and therefore likely to be promoted at work. Finally, smiling helps us stay positive. So smile![20]

29) *Tell the truth*

As is the case with smiling, so too telling the truth may have positive health benefits (not to mention the benefit to our relationships with others and thus a "successful" life). Researchers conducted an "honesty experiment," for which half the participants were instructed to stop telling lies for the 10 weeks (the average American tells about 11 lies a

---

[20] www.about.com/smiling

week). The other half served as a control group and received no such instructions. "Over the study period, the link between less lying and improved health was significantly stronger for participants in the no-lie group, who experienced, on average, approximately four fewer mental-health complaints, about three fewer physical complaints, and improvement in their close personal relationships.[21] The moral: tell the truth!

30) *Say "I love you" often* and 31) *Keep your promises*

Robert Fulghum tells a touching story of a promise made and broken. His seven year old daughter one day made his lunch and then gave him a second sack held together with tape, staples, and paper clips. She assured him he needed both sacks so he gave her a kiss and headed off to work.

During his hurried lunch he ate the sandwich and looked over the contents of the "other" sack. It contained two hair ribbons, three small stones, a plastic dinosaur, a pencil stub, a tiny seashell, two animal crackers, a marble, a used lipstick, a small doll, two chocolate kisses, and thirteen pennies. It brought a slight smile but looked like nothing more than junk. By the end of the day the entire contents of both bags ended up in the trash. That evening, Molly asked for her sack. Fulghum claimed he "left it at the office" then asked, "Why?" She handed him a note and said, "I forgot to put this note in it. Besides, I want it back."

Fulghum couldn't understand why she wanted the sack until she explained, "Those are my things in the sack, Daddy, the ones I really like. I thought you might like to play with them, but now I want them back. You didn't lose the bag, did you Daddy?" When her eyes filled with tears he promised to return it, and then the lump in his throat metastasized as he read her note which simply said, "I love you, Daddy."

---

[21] Sharon Jayson, *USA Today*, August 4, 2012

He hustled to the office and dumped the contents of his trashcan on the desk. The janitor heard his story and didn't think he was foolish. He simply said, "I got kids too." Upon his return from a successful salvage, Fulghum had his daughter tell him about each piece in the bag. It took her a long time to explain because each item had a story, dreams, and memories. A few days later, Molly trusted her daddy with the bag again and this time he treated it as the treasure it was. The exchange occurred many times over the years until one day the game ran out and she didn't ask for its return. Two decades later, this little tattered bag is one of his most treasured possessions. It reminds him of a time when he missed the affection of his little girl and forgot to cherish what was important to her.[22] Say "I love you" often, and always tell the truth.

32) *Make eye contact*

Daniel Wendler has struggled with Asperger's his entire life. He has turned his condition into a platform for putting together a web site[23] in which he suggests that it is important not only to make eye contact, but to do so appropriately. The secret to making great eye contact, says Wendler, is to match your eye contact with your conversation partner, a practice that helps your partner feel comfortable. The rules may change based on the emotional content of the conversation, and/or based on the culture background of your conversation partner.

33) *Extend a sincere greeting*

A genuinely sincere greeting takes work. It usually means stopping whatever else we're doing in order to focus on whoever it is who has entered our world. Of course, sometimes such *enterings* are more like *intrusions* which makes it all the more challenging to be sincere. But put yourself on the other side of this equation and it's easy to

---

[22] *It was on Fire When I Lay Down On It*, Robert Fulghum, 1989
[23] www.improveyoursocialskills.com

> Making other people feel truly welcome is a gift that will pay untold dividends.

understand why this is an important skill: making other people feel truly welcome is a gift to them, and will pay untold dividends in the depth of your relationships.

34) **Speak when spoken to**

Some people take this to imply that you should be quiet until you are addressed, and in times past it certainly carried that meaning. But in these days of low social capital it is amazing how frequently people simply ignore those who are speaking to them. To speak when spoken to is simply a reminder to be tuned in to others and to have the thoughtfulness to respond when addressed. Be alert, be mindful, and be civil!

35) **Do unto others as you would have them do unto you**

Jesus offers this phrase as part of the Sermon on the Mount in Matthew 7:12 (and also in Luke 6), where it completes a list of similarly impossible instructions. And while it's true that variations of the "rule of ethical reciprocity" appear across many world cultures and religions, dating back to well before the time of Jesus, it is also true that most of them use a negative phrasing of this rule ("don't do to others what you don't want them to do to you...") which is not as proactive or arguably even as demanding, especially when the rule is expressed (as it was by Christ) as "love your neighbor as yourself." In any event the prevalence of the rule strongly suggests that it is, indeed, a very important skill for living!

36) **Don't gossip**

The church gossip, and self-appointed arbiter of the church's morals, kept sticking her nose into other people's business. Several church members were unappreciative of her activities, but feared her enough to maintain their silence.

She made a mistake, however, when she accused George, a new member, of being drunk after she saw his pickup truck parked in front of the town's only bar one afternoon. She commented to George on a Sunday morning, in the company of many, that everyone seeing it there would know what he was doing. George, a man of few words, stared at her for a moment and then just walked away. He didn't explain, defend, or deny; he said nothing. Later that evening, George quietly parked his pickup in front of her house and left it there all night. Enough said.

37) *Communicate*

Good communication is, first of all, polite. Respond to people when they talk to you (see above, *Speak when spoken to*), and respond in appropriate and polite ways ("thank you," "please," and "excuse me" are good basics to start with, adding a smile might not hurt either).

Good communication continues with being attentive to the person (or people) you are communicating with. In verbal exchange this means *listening* and doing so carefully. Don't be so eager to get in what you want to say that you miss what is being said. In written exchange (like e-mails) it means *really* reading carefully...not just the first sentence...and then *re-reading* after you write your reply to make sure you answered all the questions or touched on all the relevant topics in all the right ways. Editing is the great lost art of communication.

> Editing
> is the great lost art
> of communication.

38) *Share*

Pastor and author Tom Long once told a story about a student and his father who went jogging in their suburban neighborhood. As they ran the man shared what he was learning in seminary about urban ministry, and the father, an inner city pastor, related experiences of his own ministry. Near the end of their jog they decided to phone ahead for a pizza delivery. As they headed for a pay phone, however, a homeless man approached them, asking for spare change. The father reached into the pockets of his sweat pants and pulled out two handfuls of coins. "Here," he said to the homeless man, "take what you need. The homeless man could hardly believe his good fortune. "I'll take it all," he said scooping up the coins. It only took a second for the father to realize that he now had no change for the phone. "Pardon me," he beckoned to the homeless man. "I need to make a call. Can you spare some change? The homeless man turned and held out the change. "Here," he said, "take what you need."

39) *Do no harm*

The phrase *first do no harm* is usually attributed to the Hippocratic Oath. It is actually not found there, but it is found elsewhere in the writings of Hippocrates, specifically in *Epidemics*:

*With regard to the dangers of these cases, one must always attend to the seasonable concoction of all the evacuations, and to the favorable and critical abscesses. The concoctions indicate a speedy crisis and recovery of health; crude and undigested evacuations, and those which are converted into bad abscesses, indicate either want of crisis, or pains, or prolongation of the disease, or death, or relapses; which of these it is to be must be determined from other circum-stances. The physician must be able to tell the antecedents, know the present, and foretell the future - must mediate these things, and have two special objects in view with regard to disease, namely, **to do good or to do no harm.** The art consists in three things - the disease, the patient, and the* *physician. The physician is the servant of the art, and the patient must combat the disease along with the physician.*[24]

Whether in medicine or in our relationships, the advice is sound.

40) ***Apologize when you are wrong***
Beverly Engel, author of *The Power of Apology*, shares that when she was 35 years old she divorced her mother. "I felt that under the circumstances, it was the only thing I could do," she writes. "I had long felt that she had damaged me with emotional abuse while I was growing up, and during my adulthood she continued to treat me in ways I didn't like." She continues,

I became so emotionally and physically stressed when I was with her that it affected my health. So I made the difficult yet necessary decision to stop seeing her. The estrangement lasted three years. During that time, I wrote a book titled Divorcing a Parent, *in which I told about the experience of divorcing my mother and encouraged others in similar situations to consider doing the same. Then one day the phone rang. When I picked it up the person on the other end of the line said, "I'm sorry." It was my mother. Waves of relief washed over me. Resentment, fear and anger drained out. Much to my surprise, those two simple words seemed to wipe away years of pain and bitterness. They were the words I had been waiting to hear most of my life.*

I knew that it had taken all the courage my extremely proud mother could muster to say them, so I didn't have to belabor the point. The important thing was that she was saying she was sorry—something she'd never done before. I could tell by the tone of her voice that she truly regretted the way she had treated me.

---

[24] www.ancienthistory.about.com/od/greekmedicine/f/ HippocraticOath.htlm

Of course, this was only the beginning of the story. Although I believed her apology, I didn't yet know if her behavior toward me would be different. This I tested over time. But by apologizing she had acknowledged that I had a reason to be hurt and angry, and that was extremely empowering for me.

It is incredible to realize the power we hold to free someone else when we can muster the strength to apologize. In many ways apology is the flip side of **forgiveness** (see above): it provides a release and a way forward in any relationship.

Engel suggests that there are emotional benefits in apology for both the recipient and the giver. "Research shows that receiving an apology has a noticeable, positive physical effect on the body. An apology actually affects the bodily functions of the person receiving it—blood pressure decreases, heart rate slows and breathing becomes steadier." Part of this is related to what Engel shares in her own story: when someone apologizes it validates the hurt we have been feeling. And in the one giving the apology there is a release from guilt and shame as we take responsibility for our actions, which in turn can free us from both emotional and physical burdens.

According to Engel a meaningful apology communicates the three R's: regret, responsibility and remedy.

Statement of regret for having caused the hurt or damage
  "While your intention may not have been to cause harm, you recognize that your action or inaction nevertheless did hurt this person. This regret needs to be communicated. This includes an expression of empathy with an acknowledgement of the injustice you caused."

An acceptance of responsibility for your actions
  "This means not blaming anyone else and not making excuses for what you did. For an apology to be effective it must be clear that you are accepting total responsibility for

your action or inaction. Therefore, your apology needs to include a statement of responsibility."

Statement of willingness to remedy the situation
"While you can't undo the past, you can repair the harm you caused. Therefore, a meaningful apology needs to include a statement in which you offer restitution, or a promise to take action so that you will not repeat the behavior."

"Unless all three of these elements are present," says Engel, "the other person will sense that something is missing in your apology and he or she may feel shortchanged."[25]

---

[25] www.psychologytoday.com/collections/201204/making/the-power-apology

FAITH

Once upon a time an atheist professor told his college class that he could prove there wasn't a God. He then called out, "God if you are real, then I want you to knock me off this platform. I'll give you 15 minutes!" Ten minutes went by, during which time the professor kept taunting, saying, "Here I am God, I'm still waiting"

During the last couple of minutes and a 240 pound football player happened to walk by the door and heard what the professor said. He ran into the room and hit the professor full force, sending the man flying off the platform. The professor got up, obviously shaken and said, "Why did you do that?"

The football player replied, "God was busy; He sent me!"

Not everyone has faith or sees the need for it. I can respect that but at the end of the day even atheists are making a faith statement...they *believe* there is no God. To those who have it, faith is arguably the most important skill of life, and so could have easily been the first set of skills we looked at in this series, but if you're not a person of faith I wanted you to at least read this far!

41) *PRAY**

Prayer is definitely one of the *Big Five.* To pray is nothing more, and certainly nothing less, than to talk with God, and it turns out there is really no great skill involved at all. In other words, when people invite me to pray at formal functions, or even over lunch, it has more to do with the fact that I have a lot of prayerful sounding words pretty close to the top of my vocabulary, and also with the fact that as an extrovert I am willing to talk when most sensible people will keep still. But in point of fact the one-word prayer, "Help" is just as effective a communication with God as the much fancier sounding, "O Lord, we beseech thee in all tender care and mercy, to come hither to our aide..."

No, the "skill" involved in this skill of life has nothing to do with what words we use, but only that we *do it.* It's when we try to do everything in our own strength and wisdom that we'll likely fall flat on our face. The skill involved in prayer is taking the time to talk to God—giving thanks, seeking guidance, gaining wisdom, and sharing all that concerns us

42) *Give your worries to God* and 43) *Be thankful in good times and challenging times.*

As it happens, both of these are accomplished in prayer.

So, there is no skill to praying except to do it, but there is a way to pray that seems to help build this skill. It's the very biblical practice of talking to God, giving your worries and your thanks to God, by saying things out loud and with emotion. It's not that there is anything wrong with silent prayer *per se*, it's only that too often those silent prayers wander off into a conversation with yourself. Speaking prayers out loud helps us stay focused, and saying them with emotion is really just being true to what drives them out of our hearts and to the throne of grace. If you don't mean it, or don't take it too seriously, then what is God to do with it?

Now, let me let you in on a little secret: you want to know the best place to pray this way? It's when you are driving in your car alone. If that happens to be at night, so much the better, but even in the day, no one is going to think twice if you are yelling or even crying because they'll figure you're talking on your cell or singing along to the radio. But whether in your car, or out loud, or whatever, the main thing is to pray!

> Let me let you in on a little secret: the best place to pray out loud is when you are driving in your car alone.

44) *Remain still*

This also is part of prayer, and is kind of the other side of the coin to praying out loud. Malcolm Muggeridge once wrote, "We need to find God, and he cannot be found in noise and restlessness. God is the friend of silence. See how nature trees, flowers, grass grow in silence; see the stars, the moon and sun, how they move in silence... the more we receive in silent prayer, the more we can give in our active life. We need silence to be able to touch souls. The essential thing is not what we say, but what God says to us and through us. All our words will be useless unless they come from within; words which do not give the light of Christ increase the darkness."[26]

45) *Accept God's amazing grace*

Again, something that at least sometimes is part of prayer, but is also just a way of life. Obviously many people pray without having accepted God's grace and mercy but the freedom to approach God with all our cares and concerns, the joy of giving God all our praise and thanks, are very much connected to knowing that God has freely given amazing grace to wretches just like us. And while a lot of people *think* they have accepted God's grace and mercy I can tell you from experience, both as a counselor and as a member of the human race, that many times we do not. It's particularly hard for those raised in a western capitalistic culture where you don't get somethin' for nothin'. You know, there's no free lunch, you have to pull yourself up by your own bootstraps, et cetera, et cetera. Go read the story Jesus told about the prodigal son (Luke 15). We're all prodigals, we all wander away, but God is always waiting for our return, ready to run to us with arms outstretched.

I guess that's why it's amazing!

---

[26] Malcolm Muggeridge, *Something Beautiful for God*, 1977, p 48

46) *Never stop being amazed*

It is *really* easy to become jaded and cynical as we get older, and in so doing to lose our joy in living. We said at the outset that if something is out of whack in your life it may be that you've lost track of one of these 50 basic skills. Up until now you may have been ticking off all of these—you don't gossip, you keep a budget, you manage to obey the law, you floss—but still something is out of balance, you're just not your old self. Perhaps you've lost your sense of being amazed at the world God has created for us.

Tom Bodett tells of a time when he, his wife, and his young son shared a bedroom while visiting friends. Bodett woke up early, realized he was in a strange place, and couldn't go back to sleep. This gave him a chance to hear his child wake up for the first time. That's because sleeping in the same room with his son was not their usual arrangement. Usually the first sign indication that their child was awake was the sound of him screaming from his crib. His son was at the age where he had a fairly limited vocabulary. "More," was one word that they heard the most, with "No," running a close second. The words "Hello," "bye-bye," "momma," and "daddy" made up pretty much the rest of his vocabulary, but none of these would quite get the job done as well as screaming when he woke up and wanted out of his crib.

The little boy did have one other word, very seldom used, the word "Wow." He would only say "wow" if something really impressed him, like if dad let a frying pan catch on fire and then juggled it out the front door into the snow. That would be a "wow." Or if the family was on the way into town, and the car hit a ditch and turned around backwards, that would be a "wow."

On this particular morning, Bodett was lying there in bed, too early to get up, too awake to go back to sleep, and so he started to plan his day. They'd have to pack up and get home. Once there he'd have wood to put up, a door to fix, a few letters to write, some bills to pay. His wife would clean house, and their little boy would refuse to take his nap. Luck willing, they might have a little time together before the weekend ran out and the rat race started all over again. Hardly the stuff of dreams.

As Bodett was lying there brooding over all this, he heard his little boy stir from his sleep. He rolled over, opened his eyes, and said "wow." "Suddenly," says Bodett, "I felt like a heel. With all my training to 'think good thoughts,' 'look on the bright side,' and 'take it a day at a time,' I had woken up to a near-miserable world. This little boy who knows nothing of optimism woke up, saw he had a new day, and gave it his grandest praise. I learned something. It dawned on me that this innocent little child was at the place I wanted to be. To wake up in the morning, take a look at the world, and say 'wow' is probably about as close to contentment as a person can ever hope to get."[27]

47) *Never stop being curious*

Staying amazed is related to keeping your appetite for learning new things alive. Be a life-long learner and you'll stay *both* amazed and curious. As the old commercials say, "Stay thirsty..."

48) *Read*

A huge part of staying amazed and curious is that we read. Read widely. Read daily. Read articles that are completely outside of your field (you never know what will fire up a synergy), and read for pleasure. And of course, read the Bible.

One proof that the Bible is the word of God, and the reason it has been actively studied for thousands of years, is that it stays ever fresh and new. Sometimes when we read a passage it speaks to us in deep ways, but sometimes the

---

[27] *Small Comforts*, Tom Bodett, 1987, pp 156-156

effect is delayed...because it is God's word. Read a passage that you read the year before and see it in a whole new light...because it is God's word. Read a passage and then find yourself in a situation the next day when you have just the right words, *those words,* because it is God's word.

49) *Give back*

When we give away our time, our labor, and our money we are doing more than helping someone else, we are helping ourselves. In his book *Deep Survival: Who Lives, Who Dies, and Why* Laurence Gonzales has studied why some people survive severe outdoor adventure accidents and others don't. It turns out that one predictor of survival is to be a child. No one is exactly sure why, but it may be that young children simply exist where they are and follow their instincts: if they cold, they crawl into the hollow of a tree; if they get tired, they sit down and rest; if they get thirsty, they drink (170). But if that time has passed for you then consider that the other attribute that tends to predict survival is helping someone else. Over and over again this finding came through.

> Helping someone else is the best way to ensure your own survival.

Gonzales writes, "Helping someone else is the best way to ensure your own survival. It takes you out of yourself. It helps you to rise above your fears. Now you're a rescuer, not a victim. And seeing how your leadership and skill buoy others up give you more focus and energy to persevere. The cycle reinforces itself: You buoy them up, and their response buoys you up" (180).

50) *Receive hope*

Human beings can survive a lot of things, but take away hope and the road becomes long and bleak. The Bible says that "since we are justified by faith," in other words, since we have accepted God's grace and mercy, "we have peace with God through our Lord Jesus Christ, through whom we have obtained access to this grace in which we stand; and we boast in our _hope_ of sharing the glory of God. And not only that, but we also boast in our sufferings, knowing that suffering produces endurance, and endurance produces character, and character produces _hope_, and _hope_ does not disappoint us, because God's love has been poured into our hearts through the Holy Spirit that has been given to us (Romans 5:1-5).

There's a Balkan fairy tale about a poor woman who caught a golden fish, released it, and in return gained wealth and happiness. Every Bosnian child knows this, but many years ago that story came to life as a story of hope.

In 1990, Smajo Malkoc came back from working in Austria with an unusual gift for his teen-age sons, Dzevad and Catib: an aquarium with two goldfish. Two years later the civil war came to their town. As Bosnian Serb forces advanced the women and children fled and the men tried to resist. Malkoc was killed. When his wife, Fehima, sneaked back into the destroyed village to bury her husband and take what remained of their belongings, she spotted the fish in the aquarium. She let them out into the nearby lake, thinking that perhaps they would be more fortunate than the family.

A few years later Fehima again returned to their town, this time with her sons, to find nothing but ruins. Eyes misting over, she turned toward the lake and glimpsed something strange. She got closer and was stunned to see the whole lake shining from all the golden fish in it. "I had to think of my husband," she said, "it was something he left me that I never hoped for."

It was true: during all the years of killing around the lake, life underwater had flourished. It was a gift that provided a livelihood as mother and sons began to feed and sell the fish to others. Now homes, bars, and coffee shops in the area all have aquariums with golden fish from the village lake. The Malkoc house is rebuilt from the ruins and is one of the biggest in the village. Two new cars are parked in front, and the family says it has enough money not to worry about the future. Says son Dzevad, "It was a special kind of gift from our father."[28]

---

[28] *Mobile Press Register,* Sunday June 7, 1998

AFTER-WORD

So, just to review: there are 50 skills you need to know in order to have a decent chance of success. Use these as a kind of checklist, something to refer to especially when life gets out of balance and seems to wobble a bit.

Of these 50 really important skills, five are really *really* important. The *Big Five* include *keeping a calendar, getting eight hours, keeping a budget, forgiving,* and *praying.*

And among these 50 really important skills there is also one that is really really *really* important: discipline. Discipline is the willingness to suffer in the present for a reward in the future. It is the essence of delayed gratification, understanding what you really want, what is really important in long term, big picture kinds of ways, and so making better decisions about the short term, small picture stuff. Learn to be disciplined and a lot of other things will fall into place pretty well.

And then, well, there's one other thing that I think you should know: *nothing you do, and nothing you fail to do, will make God love you any more than God already loves you through Jesus Christ.* I invite you to read that again...out loud.

So the thing to know is that accepting the love of God in Jesus isn't a skill you can learn, a burden you must bear, a set of rules you must follow, or any of a million other things people (including eager Christians) have made it out to be over the years. It is only, simply, letting God's love into your life, the love that is uniquely expressed in the words and work of Jesus Christ. To learn more sit down and read the book of Mark in one sitting (or get a copy of *The Jesus Story* which weaves together all four gospel accounts into one story). Then, if you'd like to talk more feel free to e-mail me at info@brantbaker.info

Blessings!

Other books and studies by Brant Baker

Hands-On Christianity: Eight Studies for Small Groups

Wine in the Bible: Eight Studies for Small Groups

The Gamer Bible Study: Six Studies for Teens

The Abingdon Children's Sermon Library (3 vols)(Editor)

Let the Children Play

Teaching People to Pray

The Jesus Story (with Ben Johnson)

Welcoming The Children

Let the Children Come

FIND ALL THESE, PLUS NEW PROJECTS AT

www.brantbaker.info